EMOTION-BOUND SOCIETY

A Thesis on Alternative Social Order

notionpress.com

EMOTION-BOUND SOCIETY

A Thesis on Alternative Social Order

Liladhar Pirsali

notionpress.com

Notion Press

Old No. 38, New No. 6

McNichols Road, Chetpet

Chennai - 600 031

First Published by Notion Press 2016

ISBN 978-93-5206-814-2

Email: lpirsali@gmail.com

CONTENTS

PREFACE

The thesis is a continuous thought process since my childhood focusing on 'why'. Having so many 'the great' and their thoughts and practices since time immemorial, the man is still helpless and dependent.

Globally renowned centres of 'so-called' knowledge are emphasizing on employability of man. There is no serious attempt to make him stand on his own feet. Education is still centred on rote-learning. The shackles binding him on the name of caste, creed, colour, nation and religion are tightening their grip day by day.

Why is the 'why' has not been answered so far? The beginning of the thesis starts with declaration that the answer of the question is as easy as the question itself. But, the reader has to go through the book to have a satisfactory and convincing answer!

INTRODUCTION

So much poverty, pain and suffering, helplessness, dependence and confusion, is all around that the talks on progress and achievements sound hollow. Therefore, and only therefore, I start the thesis with the basic but simple question – Why is it so that virtually all the philosophers and the philosophies, the gods and the gospels, the reformers and the reforms, the revolutionaries and the revolutions, claiming to have worked seriously to ameliorate the conditions of life, have, so far, been failure in their mission? The life is as miserable as it was in the beginning of civilization.

I dare to say that I have the answer as simple as the question itself.

But...but this 'but' is not there to complicate the answer, it is there to motivate you to read the thesis, page by page, so that no sooner do you reach the final pages, are convinced that the answer deserves your consideration; that, it gives you the status of being the master of situation. The credit goes to you for being what you are and wish to be.

Let me make it clear in the beginning itself that the language is not a perfect medium of communication. It is always governed by the physical, emotional, intellectual and spiritual conditions of the reader. Due to this, an impartial presentation has always been a challenge. And due to this again, one's responsibility counts more than anything else. It is for each and every individual to see, feel, analyze and decide so that the journey forward is of one's own choice and none other is there to be blamed for.

The life, by its very nature, is ambitious. To get birth, grow, bloom and fructify are manifestations of its growth. How to have a deserved growth is the subject matter of this treatise.

The individuals and the society are compatible to or against each other is not my problem. It is the empowerment of individual, the brick of society, I am dealing with.

INDIVIDUAL EMPOWERMENT

It starts with information

The individual empowerment starts with information. Good and bad, sensible and senseless, liked and disliked, worth and worthless, one has to have information about. No serious thing in or about life is possible in vacuum. There must be a base and the pieces of information are the base. It is the information which makes one feel that the world is larger than one's perception and provides far more opportunities quite beyond the perceived limits.

ANALYSIS OF INFORMATION

But, having a large number of pieces of information itself is not sufficient. There are only a few of them which are useful. Therefore, analysis of the information is essential. Analysis leads to knowledge.

INFORMATION AND KNOWLEDGE

Before proceeding further, let us examine the words information and knowledge. The sugar is sweet, so is the milk. This is information. The sweetness of sugar and that of milk is not the same. The difference is related to taste. The knowledge knows the difference.

KNOWLEDGE TO BE COPULATED WITH DREAMS

But the knowledge is barren. It does not produce anything by itself. To make it useful, it is to be copulated with dreams. One may call it vision, ambition, aspiration, ideal, wish or even pipedream. The dream is to be realized in future but demands action right now. It is the moving force and its velocity depends upon one's clarity of knowledge. Better the clarity, clearer the dream and faster the speed towards its realization.

WORK IS TIRESOME

The work, physical or mental or of any other kind, is tiresome. Harder the work, more tiring it is. Nothing valuable is achieved without hard work. The total body is involved in it; all the organs, the organs of action, the sense organs, the reflexive and motor nerves, the mind and each hair of the body and its exclusive world. More the involvement, additional is the tiredness. One is busy all the time. Twenty four hours a day are never sufficient. Seven days in a week, three hundred and sixty-five days in a year, each of the moments is a busy schedule for a hard worker.

HARD WORK PRESUPPOSES PHYSICAL FITNESS

Any hard work presupposes physical fitness. It is the body and body alone which is the basic means for an action. The healthy body is the strongest defense against all types of onslaughts against life. It is the only resort of a sound mind too.

Only a sound mind takes up a long and hazardous journey of life. It does not waver and is capable of focusing on targets.

HOW TO HAVE A HEALTHY BODY AND A SOUND MIND

How to have a healthy body and a sound mind is a challenge throughout the ages. Of course, there cannot be a full and final answer, but the exercises which cover-up the totality of one's being are helpful. Most existing civilizations have developed their systems helpful for such exercises. The Indian system of Yoga is one of them. It is an exercise, rather a group of drills, for body and mind, for outer and inner organs, sensory and nervous system, emotional and intellectual layers of existence. It is not complicated and can be mastered by little practice.

WORK IS ESSENTIAS AND ONE HAS TO LIKE IT

It is common knowledge that no living being can sit idle. But the work is tiresome. Even the pastimes are so. To work without feeling tired depends upon the liking of it.

I have heard an allegory. Once there was a pilgrim passing through a huge construction site. It was the summer sun shining overhead. His curiosity forced him enter the site. He saw a large number of workers engaged in breaking stones. They were profusely sweating. He approached one of the groups of workers and enquired them of their work. The irritated workers started abusing him for not being sympathetic to their sad plight of working under the scorching sun. He preferred to hastily go away from there. After a hundred steps ahead, he came across another group of laborers doing the same job. Instead of anger, their faces reflected deep sadness. After enquiry, they revealed that stone-breaking was their profession and irrespective of the climate, they have to do it. They refused to talk further. But after a few scores of steps ahead, a surprise was awaiting for him. Though the group, too, was busy with stone breaking, each member's face was shining and full of joy. They themselves wanted to share their happiness with the traveler. They told him, "We are not ordinary stone breakers. We are the chosen ones constructing the abode of god! People say, he is the creator but we are the builders of his house. What a great opportunity we have and we are naturally elated!"

STRONG FAITH IN ONESELF

So much in eulogy of the work one likes. To work but not to feel tired presupposes a strong faith in oneself. Yes, the faith can accomplish miracles.

TIME-BOUND PROGRAMME

To keep the faith intact in challenging circumstances is a test one has to undergo. Lack of it or a weak one takes away the person from the chosen path. Life is too short to afford many a start. The conscientious part of it is shorter. Work is vast. Its dimensions are multifarious. One cannot do everything. Even to fulfill a single task is difficult. There is no time to go astray for a moment. Therefore, for any accomplishment, one has to act systematically, according to a time-bound program.

SELF-DISCIPLINE IS THE KEY

It is somewhat amazing that most people have developed a habit of submission. J.J. Rousseau argues that man is born free but everywhere he is in chains.

I find it otherwise. The man is, more than any other animals, born a slave with ample opportunities to realize freedom. The freedom lies in his self-discipline and his being responsible for his actions. It is like a government of oneself for oneself and by oneself. A self-disciplined person does not seek alibis. He enjoys freedom even when he is in shackles. Such ones are the pillars of a happy and contented social order.

SELF DISCIPLINE NEEDS WILL-POWER

Self-discipline needs will-power to face the challenges of life. Every action, minor or major, can be accomplished successfully by will-power alone. Success is never a fluke. The will power is the higher layer of one's existence. Every action demands will power for its execution. Stronger the will power, surer is the realization of hopes.

HOPE IS THE MOVING FORCE

Hope is the moving force in a person, a driving force of the body and the mind. The state of hopelessness results in inaction. In its extremity, it leads to suicide. The life exists because of hope. It is catalytic and overcomes death.

FAITH HELPS

In ordinary parlance, death is the end of life. There are philosophies which plead otherwise. I do not have any comments to offer. But, the faith in the continuity of existence does help in long-term planning. It is a fact that one's transformation into one's offspring is a reality and the fruits of one's actions are reaped by the following generations. No sensible person is cruel to one's children. This is quiet a plausible argument in favor of eternal life. The wish to live after death is one of the powerful catalysts for life.

WORK IS VAST, TIME IS LIMITED; SLEEP-HOURS HAVE THE ANSWER

Work is vast. Its ramifications are unlimited. Time is short and limited. How to accomplish something tangible within limited time under one's disposal has been a constant problem throughout the ages. The answer lies in sleep hours. But the modern scientists stress upon the necessity of about nine hours of sleep for the children and about eight for the adults. It is a common knowledge that the Indian tradition of education, where the retired persons used to conduct seminaries, known as Gurukuls, had hardly three to four hours left for taking complete rest. The ascetic scholars, known as Brahmacharis, used to go to bed late in the night as the tradition was to sleep after the preceptor went to bed. They had to get up early to be readied for the fire sacrifice presided over by the teacher. Usually the sacrifice was performed in Brahma-Muhoorta, i.e., the time before dawn. The scholars had to make all the preparations for it, from collecting fresh fire wood to applying cow dung to the sacrificial place. They had to get up quite early in the morning. There were hardly three to four hours left for rest. In ancient Athens and Greece, according to the description of Plato and other contemporary scholars and later in the writings of J. J. Rousseau, especially in his classical treatise on education, Emile, almost all the educationists of ancient and medieval world have suggested quite fewer hours for sleep. My enquiries from medical personnel have also revealed that eight to nine hours of sleep is quite a bookish suggestion. With my own experience as a student and later as a teacher, I am in favor of four to five hours only. It can be stretched to six hours. If this suggestion is taken seriously and implemented, one can add minimum two to three hours to one's working time.

LEADERSHIP

So far the discussion is on empowering man. It is equally important to enable society to be strong, happy and content in itself. Of course, all the members of a social whole cannot be equal in every respect. Inequality is natural. Some are born leaders and others subjects. Some are naturally masters, others obedient servants. Some like to lead, others to follow. The notion of equality is an idea, which in action is to be an honorable member of the social whole. It is an opportunity to act freely and participate in social intercourse. In reality, a person is just a cog in a wheel and the social apparatus is composed of innumerable wheels with countless cogs. In a healthy society each of the cogs is important as much as any of the wheels. Whether one likes it or not, the competition is a basic instinct of any organism. It is as natural as hunger. Therefore, a society composed of various types of members, often antagonistic in their relationships, demands a philosophy of happy growth. In empowerment of an individual, the social foundation for happy growth is there. But how to empower an individual is the subject-matter of leadership.

LEADER LEADS AND IS AWARE OF HIS ROLE AND VISION

The leader leads. Whether it is a family of two or a large household, a colony, a village or a country or the world at large, there is need of a leader everywhere.

A leader is a person aware of his role and has a clear vision of what to realize. But, if the followers are novice and have little knowledge of what actually the leader stands for, it is a dangerous situation. In the long run, it leads to nowhere and the parties concerned repent for their movement. Thus, a lot of energy, resources and time are consumed. It is, therefore, necessary that the gist of the mission should percolate to each of the followers. All together should feel the same, have a wish to act united and enjoy the fruits and share the sufferings together.

LEADERSHIP IS AN ART AND A SCIENCE, TOO

The leadership is an art which deals with animate objects in the form of human beings. To convert the mass of people into comrades is a science, too. It requires thorough knowledge of administration as well as an efficient grasp of individual and group capacities, minds and psychology. The leader must be conversant with practical logic so that he can dive deep to the source of power and rise up to feel the goal of his mission. No vague ideas will be helpful. Everything should be crystal clear in the mind of the leader.

LEADER IS NOT A BOSS; HE IS A FRIEND, PHILOSOPHER AND GUIDE

The leadership is a social phenomenon and as such its variations are many, often contradictory. The leader deals with them accordingly. In doing so, the successes and the failures do not carry much importance. The actions do. A successful leader is he who keeps his followers hopeful and busy pursuing the cause united. A leader is not a boss. He is a friend, philosopher and guide. He has full respect for deliberations of his followers and possesses enough courage and guts to face their emotions, feelings and whims. His discerning capabilities make him worthy to be followed. When the mission is being pursued on the right path, the leader shows his usefulness by being absent from the track so that the led avail of the opportunity to collect enough courage to move on. The moment the journey seems derailing, he is there to hold the reign in his hand. A healthy society gives an impression to each of its members that each one is the cause and the effect of the movement of social whole.

FREEDOM DEVELOPS INTO LEADERSHIP

Man is born a slave to earn his freedom. The natural growth sheds off slavery gradually and brings in freedom. Ultimately the freedom develops into leadership traits and one turns up to be a leader oneself and thinks about others too and acts to help them. This is a natural development.

WORTHY LEADER SHARES THE SUCCESS AND OWNS THE FAILURE

It is a common experience that in successful operations all the concerned vie with each others to own the credit of the success. This often leads to individual agony and social chaos. It is, therefore, a worthy leader shares the success with the led and owns the responsibility of failure. It may sound bizarre but in the long run it turns out to be a strong base for leadership. The leader comes up as a dependable person and commands better hold on the masses.

A leader is a director behind the curtain. On the stage he is the main actor and amongst the audience, he is one of them. Behind the scene, he is a king-maker; on the front, a General. Among the subjects, he is one of them; if older, a reverend, if younger, more lovable than others.

MAN AND SOCIAL ORDERS

Rationalism has led man to a stage where arrangements for his welfare are turned into shackles. He is being crushed by lifeless machines of his own manufacture. The ideals of life put forth look great while judged by reason. In actual practice, they demand controlled environment. The question arises whether he should accept it as the ultimate destiny of his being or work for a better future. In my assumption, a meaningful life is possible in a social order based on nature.

STATE IS NOT NATURAL

The living organism has always desired to live a happy and contented life. Man is not an exception to it. To make his journey comfortable he seeks protection and other facilities. The institutions, including family, state. etc., are manifestations of this search for contentment. Whereas the family is natural in its formation, state is not so. Some cunning people inspired by selfish motives contrived to exploit natural instinct of fear and wish for protection of man, founded state. Responding to man's desire for protection, they enrolled police and army. Man's inertia to labor and irresponsible attitude towards his actions persuaded them to propagate that even little labor and lack of responsibility can make him happy and content. The system, thus devised, started showing off its true color in course of time. The man was subjected to suppression. He resisted it. But it was too late. The so called protective police and army began crushing his resistance. When the exploitation turned intolerable, man waged 'revolutions'. The exploiters clandestinely declare themselves as revolutionaries and took the reign of man's destiny in their hands. It is noteworthy that even after so many 'successful' movements the fate of man has not changed. The scarcity of means of livelihood, tremendous increase in human population, miraculous scientific progress and tightening grip of exploitative system are turning situation worse day by day.

Before proceeding ahead with the thesis let me give a glimpse of theories of state since very inception of civilization. This brief sketch will also offer an opportunity to the readers to delve into the mind of the author.

The systems of governments, though not in chronological order, according to the status of the rulers and the ruled, have been as the rule by the one, by the few and by all.

INERT PEOPLE AND RULE BY ONE

The inert people while away their time in eating and merry-making. They have little foresight. They deserve to be ruled by a king or a dictator. Political scientists observe that that type of social order was a reality in the beginning of civilization. It is always practiced with the people of that sort of nature.

COMPETITION FOR LEADERSHIP AND THE GOVERNMENT BY THE FEW

In course of time, with the development of awakening among the masses, more and more persons aspired to be rulers and some of them succeeded. As a result, aristocracies and oligarchies came into existence. Many a semi-developed people are still being governed by such systems.

AWAKENED PEOPLE AND THE RULE BY ALL

A people cannot always remain sleepy or inert. They have to wake up, especially in societies where the rulers are cruel or the natural progress forces people to reevaluate their social values. The ideas of democracy, socialism, communism and Sarvodaya or the good of all are the result of such development.

IN DEMOCRACIES THE REPRESENTATIVES USURP POWER

In democracies, on the name of the people, their representatives usurp power and execute their selfish agenda. They hold mock periodic elections to justify their position. On the name of instant welfare, they execute short term plans. The real good of the people stands neglected. It was Karl Marx who tried to give words to the hypocritical and deceitful behavior of the representatives, their selfishness and unprincipled actions on the name of common good. He gave a clarion call to the workers of the world to unite and fight against such system. Since the labor is the prime force for all types of production, the workers united could keep a hold on exploitative system.

DISILLUSIONMENT FROM COMMUNISM

But, Communism, the social system propagated as an embodiment of an ideal way of life, has disillusioned man. The representatives of the toiling masses are not only equally crafty, hypocrites and selfish, their behavior is unrestrained and autocratic. It was first time in human history that a strong mortar wall was erected to divide a people on the line of ideologies. The communist rulers not only ruled politically, they even interfered in moral, social and spiritual activities of the people. Any resistance to their authority invited ruthless punishment.

It does not mean that Communism has no positive contributions. In the history of mankind, it was the first large scale movement to accord dignity to human labor. But the Communist rule could not do away weaknesses of the social orders it volunteered to overthrow.

SOCIALISM AND MAN'S MORAL DEGRADATION

The philosophy of Karl Marx could not bring desired results. Then, the half-hearted thinkers came into existence. They were not prepared to delve into the depth of life but interested in drawing the best from all the extremes. On the one hand they preferred liberty of democracy and on the other approved of the tenets of the theories of organization put forth by Karl Marx and the like. Propagated as Socialism, it has no practical theory of its own. The hollow and impractical idealism of Socialism created inferiority psychosis in man.

SARVODAYA NEGATES HUMAN NATURE

A possibility of better social order named as Sarvodaya or the good of all was envisaged by M. K. Gandhi and Vinoba Bhave in India. After shaking off its slavery from the 'democratic' Great Britain and enriched by the experience of Communist revolution in Russia, India could have examined the practicability of Sarvodaya. But the word is in vogue since so long nothing tangible has come up so far. The Indian political leadership has used it as a stepping stone to realize its selfish and sectarian ambitions. Binoba Bhave clung to the philosophy of Sarvodaya in his whole life, but could not change its utopian character. However, the reader must read Vinoba's 'Swarajya Shastra' (The Science of Self Rule), a political treatise advocating establishing a good social order. The book is as honest as 'Republic' of Plato, 'Social Contract' of Jean Jacques Rousseau, 'Communist Manifesto' of Karl Marx, 'Hind Swaraj' (The Self Rule for India) of M. K. Gandhi and 'Integral Humanism' of Deen Dayal Upadhyay, the other great classics on political philosophy.

But neither the honesty nor the high sounding words or slogans are sufficient to ameliorate the condition of life. The drawbacks in the very thought processes need to be examined, understood, explained, and corrected.

MISTAKE

Even today we assume that only a few people are capable to rule. The existing political systems support it. The system of election based on adult franchise corroborates it. On the name of discipline, the authority is vested in the few, who in turn hold leadership in their hands and embark upon fulfilling their personal selfish agenda together with their cronies and flatterers. None has given any serious thought to a system where man is supreme and his own destiny maker. Even the Sarvodayites' emphasis upon decentralization to the village level with all-powerful village council is practically an attempt to divide society into the ruler and the ruled. Of course, there are differences among men and women on physical, emotional, intellectual and spiritual grounds. But the weak has no emancipation except in submission before the powerful is derogatory and a disgrace to human personality.

Is there a single person who does not wish to be his own master? Or, who prefers to be ruled by others? But, at the same time, he wants to boss others. Should there be any restraint on this nature of his? Since, everyone in some way or the other, wants to be a ruler, no one should obstruct this aspiration of others by force. But the word 'should' has moral connotations. The need is of a philosophy of life where the force itself loses its force of forcing others.

TOWARDS A GOOD SOCIAL ORDER

RESPONSIBLE MAN

The responsible man deserves to have a good social order.

What is responsibility? It is accountability to oneself as well as to the social whole in one's thoughts, words and deeds. Is it against selfishness? An act for one's pleasure or satisfaction is termed as selfish. Of course, the laborer looks selfish as he utilizes his wages for his livelihood. But, a professor draws enough salary to live a happy and contented life. Still, he is busy day in and day out in persuading his thesis. The hungry mother feeds the child first. Is the ascetic not trying to fathom the depth of his own self? Then, why to blame selfishness? The need is not to get rid of it or make it a stepping stone for progress but be responsible enough for one's selfish acts. This is the subject-matter of this treatise on social order.

KNOWLEDGE OF EXPLOITATION

The first step towards a good social order is the knowledge of the practice of exploitation. One has to know the expansion of it. At the same time one has to be aware of one's explicit or implicit support to it.

The authorities are misleading man because he has no courage to stand erect and fight against injustice. He is poor and deprived of his dues because he has accepted it as his destiny. The machines are crushing him because he allows himself to be crushed. His personality depends upon submitting himself to the system of exploitation. Blaming others for it will not solve the problem.

RAMIFICATION OF EXPLOITATION

The story of exploitation makes the hair stand on its end. On the one hand, the necessities for life cost excessively in comparison of their actual cost of production. On the other, the rightful wages of the unorganized workforce are slashed to the bare minimum of the survival level. The organized labor is won over by emoluments unjustifiable by any logic. At a time when per capita income of the country is barely purchasable, the organized worker draws a monthly salary in five or six digits.

The taxes are omnipresent. Their collection is systematically organized. The amount, thus, collected is monopolized in the hands of exploiters and spent on their whims. In the process, a major portion is grabbed by them. According to one of the Prime Ministers of 'democratic' India, only ten percent of the sanctioned government funds reach the targeted beneficiaries. The rest is pocketed by the middlemen. It is an open secret that a person, as soon as he grabs authority, his movable and immovable property sky-jumps many folds.

Do you ever ask the question why a Pakistani or a Chinese national is your enemy? Is he inflicting any harm upon you on his own free will? Do you really desire to kill him? Of course, all the answers are in negative. Then, why is he your enemy? He is so because the propaganda machinery centered in the hands of exploiters is creating the enemy-psychosis. You are brainwashed to accept their logic. The presence of the police and the military is to enforce their dictates. The constitution, the laws, the rules and regulations, almost all the arrangements of the so-called civil society are basically for the protection of the interest of the exploiters. They have very little or no use for common man.

Sometimes the common man is exploited on the name of political isms, other times, on the names of caste, creed, religion, state or language or ways of living. Sometimes it may be just on the name of 'my village' or 'my hamlet'. But he is the sufferer every time, all the times!

As per the propaganda, the police force is there for the protection of common citizen. Ask any common man to move the police station for registering a crime against him. He will tell you how much helpful the police are! How can a force created to protect the interest of the exploiters be a friend of a common man?

The tax-system, evolved to create resources for running a so-called welfare state, is used to strengthen the hold of the powerful over the common masses. All the useful goods are taxed at innumerable points and the collected amount is disbursed on their whims. The powerful have final say in every sphere of life. They tell you how many children one should produce. It is they who decide when, how and what the children should learn. They direct you whether you accept or reject the mysteries of life. You have just to obey. If, by chance, any one from the exploited tries to acquire sufficient strength to face their injustice, they collectively do everything to destroy him. Or, if failed in doing so, their next strategy is to win over or force him to their side. At such occasions, they adopt the policy of dividing, threat, bribery and persuasion in reverse order. At first, they persuade him not to go against them. If he looks steadfast to his position, they bribe him to stop go further. Even then if he does not submit to their will, they put him in trouble or try to annihilate him. If it, too, does not work, they create schism in his life. Even if he is still not submissive, they try to make friends with him to win over to their fold.

In spite of all this, I do say that the powerful are not responsible for exploitation! Who is there not interested in taking benefit of others? It is the responsibility, the total one, of man that he allows them to do so. If he decides so, he can stop it. At the first step, he has to be aware of the way the exploitation is carried on.

IDENTIFICATION OF THE EXPLOITER

Now, let us describe the second step towards a good social order. It is the identification of the exploiter. The exploiter may be an individual, a group of people, an institution or an organization. It may be even the so-called welfare state! After identification, the knowledge of the method and vocabulary of the exploiter is essential.

THE EXPLOITER

A person who eats without putting in necessary labor is an exploiter. A person who consumes more than the value of his labor is, to that extent, an exploiter. The rule of nature is that everyone should work sufficiently for one's living. The child cannot perform productive labor. The milk in the mother's breast is there to compensate for it.

How to fix-up the value of one's labor? A farm-worker, after putting in hard labor of minimum ten hours, gets hardly thirty rupees. A teacher earns about four to six hundred rupees in just four hours' labor. The manager or the director of a firm earns a few thousands daily. This kind of illogical differences will disappear with the awakening of man.

Whereas a man as laborer wishes to be compensated the most for his labor, as a consumer he wants to pay the least. This contradiction can be resolved in a competitive society of awakened people. It has potentiality of putting a break on exploitation.

METHODS OF EXPLOITATION

How strange is it that the so-called mentors, instead of persuading the scientists to invent methods of recycling abundant rotten and discarded materials around, including human excreta and urine, are promoting costly and harmful chemical fertilizers! They are oblivious of the fact that many an interesting farmer is producing better crops by using organic manure. The exploiters are promoting tractors, not bullocks and ploughs. They are neglecting the value of abundant sunlight and wind-power and promoting thermal or atomic energy. Of course, the quantity of work performed by sophisticated machines is more and the cost of production is minimized. But a world reeling under unemployment, the use of machines is a bane in disguise. What a height of madness is it that the abundance of sunlight and wind-power is neglected at the cost of thermal or atomic energy! The organized mainstream workforce is bribed in the form of illogical high wages. The large number of workers of the unorganized sector does not get sufficient for bare survival. The money which is siphoned off thus used to strengthen the mechanism of exploitation.

Do you get the bank loan easily? What do you have to pawn for? Who is there to be your guarantor? As a citizen you may argue that you, too, have a share in national capital. Who is there to listen to it? Of course, to subdue the resentment, some of you are served with the leftovers.

Where there is not sufficient coarse cloth to cover the toiling masses, the banks are lending public money to the mills manufacturing fine cloths. When there are not enough earthen pots for all, the stainless steel industry is bestowed with innumerable favors. How much to elaborate the ways of exploitation!

THEIR POLICY OF EDUCATION

Such is their system of education that it generates helplessness. More the person educated, worse his dependence! An uneducated person has better chances of standing on his feet and preserving his pride and dignity. But no sooner is he educated, he turns up servile and licks the boots of his tormentors.

What is the syllabus for education? The contents of the subjects are remotely related to the life and its challenges. A person is forced to spend prime time of his life to acquire it. Is he not being trained in laziness and be a parasite? The youth who seeks challenges and enjoys adventures, is forced to sit behind the closed doors and mug-up given texts. After receiving his educational credentials, he turns up worse than a beggar. A beggar does possess a begging bowl which can be exchanged for some eatables, but the printed degree certificates holder has no such possession. He ends up as a contract laborer and is governed by market policy of hire and fire, without any guarantee for future.

And teachers, their educational certificates carry more weight than their experience. No wonder, at the age of sixty years, which is the prime age of matured experience, they are forced to retire. When they are rich only with bookish knowledge, they teach!

The engineering institutions belch out engineers with shallow creativity. The so-called specialist medical practitioners are adept in writing prescriptions only. They have little knowledge of medicinal value of the goods and facilities around.

VOCABULARY OF EXPLOITERS

The exploiters have given strange meanings to the words of daily use.

'Physical labor' is the most hated phrase in their language. Such is their abhorrence of physical labor that they are ashamed of washing their own vessels. Their hate for physical labor compels them to go for machines even for day to day work. It would have been a blessing had the machines been helpful in sorting out residual work after all the idle hands are full of it. But, on the one side, there is no sufficient employment to keep all the hands engaged, on the other side, automatic machines are replacing human labor. Some are idle because of paucity of work, some others do not like to work because it hurts their self-esteem, and the rest are turned jobless by the machines. These jobless people are fighting among themselves. They are fighting on the names of religion, literature, music, art, spirituality, etc.

The exploiters have divided world in their fiefs and termed them as 'nations'. The employment-hungry common man is engaged to protect their fiefdoms on the name of patriotism. I am really puzzled with the knowledge that a person born in a remote village of Tamilnadu in the southern Indian peninsula has the boundary of his motherland at the post number 'X' in the remote Himalayas, not beyond that! Is there no Indian culture in Pakistan, Afghanistan, Myanmar, Thailand, Malaysia or China or Nepal? Are there no red Indians in America? Is the man, irrespective of time and space, basically a child of Manu and Shraddha? But, their propaganda channels do not vouch for such arguments.

The cheat is named as clergy, the crafty as leader, member of an orthodox sect as saint. To pursue one's self interest is termed as social service and the annihilation activities are named as developmental programs.

EXPLOITER AND THE AWAKENED

There is a need, at the second step, to analyze anger against the exploiter. It is but natural that a sensible man gets furious as soon as he is aware of various methods of exploitation. He retaliates through violence. He thinks he has no alternative to it. But, an awakened man cannot be so immature to do so.

To kill an enemy is a negative attitude, a pleasure of annihilation. To fulfill the real self-interest, cooperation of the opponent is also essential.

With the strong will and determination, man takes up the next and final step. Now he creates the desired system, a dream he is contemplating since time immemorial.

NON-COOPERATION WITH THE EXPLOITER AND REJECTION OF THE MEANS EMPLOYED IN THE SYSTEM OF EXPLOITATION

The important steps for an alternative social order are non-cooperation with the exploiter and the rejection of the means employed by them.

FORCE UNDER THE COMMAND OF THE EXPLOITER IS MANNED BY YOUR OWN KITH AND KIN, WILL NOT LIKE TO BE WITH THE EXPLOITER

The exploiter, who commands coercive power enjoying common wealth surreptitiously, will suppress the challenges to his authority. He has the necessary force under his command. But the police and the military, equipped with dangerous weapons and under the command of the exploiter, are manned by your own kith and kin. No sooner do they realize their negative role, they will change side and be with their own people. They are young, capable of fulfilling responsibilities, will not like to be with the tormentors.

Yes, the members of the exploiters, too, man the police and the military force. But they are not compelled to drill with the loaded sacks. Instead, they don the uniform and officers' batches and while away their times in officers' mess. They always remain scores of kilometers away from the trouble spots, taking credit for the victory and blaming subordinates for the defeat.

PRODUCTION OF USELESS GOODS NOT PRACTICAL IN A GOOD SYSTEM

Today many a mill and factory is producing useless goods and the agricultural farms unnecessary crops only because a fake demand is created by propaganda channels. An awakened man is aware of this and he will not be a prey to their gimmicks and produce unnecessary things.

CHEAPER IS THE COST OF GOODS IN EMOTION-BOUND SOCIETY

Thousands are the means of exploitation! The ordinary mill cloth costing Rs. 20 per meter sounds normal. The emotion-bound society purchases a major portion of it. Outwardly, no exploitation is visible there. But, is there sufficient work for all the hands of yours? If some hands are idle, let them produce the necessary goods. Any purchase of it from outside at any cost is supportive to exploitation. To avoid it, produce the cloth yourself. Grow cotton-wool, spin it, weave it; all the related activities should be handled by the members of emotion-bound society. No taxes can be levied on such operations. There is a total absence of brokers, the main factor responsible for enhancing the cost of production. This is a practical alternative and can be adopted for all types of necessary and comfort goods.

TAX IS REAL POWER OF AN EXPLOITATIVE SYSTEM

All the goods, useful or otherwise, are taxed directly or indirectly. The tax is real power in the hands of exploiters. They use it in hiring and firing the police and the army, manufacturing guns and ammunitions, including bombs and atomic weapons. They create fear-psychosis for justifying their action. Are a people an enemy of another people? It is a fact that the man is basically peace loving as well as quarrelsome. But it is not natural that a group of men is an enemy to another group. The battle at the borders of the nations is certainly not between two peoples, but between the groups of exploiters for the control of resources.

MISLEADING TERMINOLOGY

The exploiters have coined some beautiful words for misleading common man. Nation, national pride, national character, motherland, etc. are baits to trap him in emotional jargon. The phrases like people's welfare are conveniently used for justifying the loot by the state on the name of people's welfare.

AWAKENED MAN WILL NOT PAY TAXES

The awakened man will not pay taxes. He cannot be a party to the system of exploitation. But, now onwards, be on the alert! With the non- payment of taxes, he has challenged the authority of statehood. The state is not an ordinary exploiter which can be scared by an ordinary boycott or power- play of common folks.

As far as indirect taxes are concerned, the consumer pays them with the price of the goods he purchases. By making alternative arrangements, he can avoid the payment, without confronting the state. But, direct taxes are collected openly. Non-payment of them invites punitive action. As a result, even the hard-earned property of a tax-evader can be confiscated. He can be arrested and put behind the bars.

FACE TO FACE STRUGGLE WITH THE STATE IS INEVITABLE

With the first step towards an alternative system, the awakened man has to be aware of the fact that one day or the other, a struggle with the monster state is inevitable.

VICTORY IS ASSURED

To assure the victory in the battle, an example is sufficient. The motivated insurgent tribal groups of Nagaland in India have turned up as headache for the powerful Indian state for decades. The numerical strength of the Naga fighters is hardly three thousand men and women. This meager number has disturbed the sleep of an all-powerful Indian state! The tribal neither have sophisticated weapons for combat, not excellent training in warfare. What they have is determination to fight to the finish and it looks that they are inching ahead towards success.

FIGHT AGAINST AND WIN OVER

The man in his first step against exploitation has to be aware that one day or the other he has to fight face to face against the almighty state. But it is not necessary that he takes up sword in his hand. As per the need, his war-strategies may include even the measures of peaceful non-cooperation with the state. He has to fight against and win over the state! Negatively, he has to stop enrolling himself in the police force or the army and positively, to adopt all kinds of strategies helpful in weakening the exploiters.

BASELESS IS THE FEAR OF ANARCHY (LAWLESSNESS)

The fear is there that the non-cooperation with the existing state machinery may lead to anarchy. But, it is not correct. We do not bring up our children because of the fear of state. Or, pay respect to elders because the police are forcing us to do so. We share the joys and sorrows of our neighborhood willingly or otherwise and are ready to sacrifice time and energy and other resources for it. The various individual and social enterprises are executed by us willingly. Most of the hard labor is done without any fear of state. The celebration at the birth of a new born, the weeping and crying at the death of beloved ones are spontaneous responses and do not require force as catalyst. We do not register a complaint at the police station or move a court after every objectionable transaction of money or quarrel or fight. We ourselves decide the rules and regulations of cohabitation and abide by them and take necessary precautions against infringement. Then, where is the need of state? The task executed by the police and the army can equally be performed by the youth force of ours. To expect state do it is submission to dependence and slavery. The awakened man's wakefulness is his armor. He is an emperor in his emotion-bound society.

INVADER IS THE EXPLOITER

How will the country be saved from foreign invasions? The phrases, 'my nation', 'other countries', etc. are the clichés used by the exploitative system. Man, by birth, is attached to his emotion-bound society and beyond that everyone or everything is superficial. The outsider, being so, may try to seduce him. If he is not ready to be exploited, no frightening or even killing will succeed. The natural bonds are glued together with self. The man is social animal because of the emotional relations.

He cannot be attached, in the same way, to the outsiders, persons or state.

INDUSTRIES TO BE RUN BY ENTERPRENEURS

If there is no state, what will happen to the large enterprises of post and telegraph, railways and shipping? Such industries, because of their large size alone, do not anticipate any state for their existence and running. Even today, a number of such ventures, in a large number of countries, are in the hands of individuals or groups and are being run successfully.

CURRENCY CIRCULATION THROUGH BANKS

How will the circulation of the currency be managed? Are the small countries not having their own currencies? The banks can manage it better. The IT industries have already given a clue for that. Even today a number of transactions ore done in similar ways.

AN EMOTION-BOUND SOCIETY IS FAVORABLE TO MAN'S NATURE AND TEMPERAMENT

The food is an essential need of life. The farmers are the producers. They live in the villages. As far as necessities are concerned, the villagers are self-dependent. They can survive without the cities. But, the cities, by nature, are dependent on villages.

Today, the cities command more respect. The condition of villages is so pathetic that there is even no sufficient potable water available there! All the essential food items are transported to the cities. It is a fact that with the awakening of man, the cities will grow weaker.

But they will not disappear. They will remain as centers for bartering of goods and industrial products, but lose the status as the hubs of social life.

At present the industrialist is selling his produce at a value many times more than the cost of production. At the same time, the farmer is seldom getting the cost price for his produce. The awakening among the people will change it. Consequently, the villages will get back their lost recognition. In brief, it can be said that the future social system will be the first such order which will be favorable to man's nature and temperament. I name it an emotion-bound society.

MEANINGFUL EDUCATION IS PREGNANT WITH SUCH A SOCIAL ORDER

Education means learning. But, what is the purpose behind learning? Without any thoughtful answer, it becomes learning anything without an aim. In fact the meaning of education is directly related to life. Why we should live, not commit suicide even in acute suffering, demands answer. It is life alone which gives the answer.

PURPOSE OF LIFE

Has life any purpose? The question itself is a challenge even to the men of letters. Is it so difficult to identify it? In fact, whatever an awakened person decides worth pursuing is the purpose. It may be anything, from food to eternal bliss.

AWAKENING

What is awakening? The ability to perceive one's self interest is awakening. Whatever one does is doing so for his 'I'. But, if someone is accumulating wealth for consumption, he is derided as selfish. If some Buddha or Mahavir renounces the kingdom for the sake of achieving enlightenment, he does not seem doing so for selfish ends. Does this renunciation not give personal satisfaction to him? The self is in a different garb, more satisfying than grabbing wealth.

The awakened man is aware of his selfishness. But, he is not fanatical, sacrificing his life for one-sided self-interest. Is it not an utter madness that a person needing hardly Rs. 500 for a month's contented living is busy in earning Rs. 5000? At the end of his life, he may have sufficient money but no contentment. The awakened man is not one-sided.

MODERN EDUCATION

MERE TRAINING FOR ACQUIRING MATERIAL WEALTH

What does a contemporary student learn? In so-called civil societies, the total education is just training in how to cultivate material wealth. Arts, music and philosophies are treated as means of earning money.

KNOWLEDGE IS ONE-SIDED

What a sad state the education is entangled in! The students doing graduation cannot even read and write correctly in their mother tongue. They just mug up a few chapters of the subject, have little inkling of it. They neither have any knowledge of life nor try to have it. Since their parents lead the contemporary society, their one-sided knowledge is termed as specialization. Conditions are created for the recognition of such learning.

TRAINING IN IDLENESS AND WASTING TIME

In fact, in today's world, the student gets training in idleness. From the age of four years to the age of 20–25, he gets such training. He sits in a walled class room under prison-like discipline and supervision. What does a student achieve after that? He gets some information, some indirect knowledge. As soon as he comes out of this web of so-called education, the challenges of life are there to face. Except a few, others run away from them and seek help in submission. Those who cannot get it, their high profile degrees are of little use.

EXPERIMENTS AT BHAVDHARA ACADEMY

Is it worth spending an important phase of life just for learning reading and writing and collecting a little information? We conducted certain experiments at our Bhavdhara Academy at Virar in Thane district of Maharashtra (India). We found that a child of 10 years of age, eager to learn and devoting two hours daily for six months was in no way less educated than the child who joined school at the age of four years and was a full timer. Recently we conducted another experiment for 5th, 6th and 7th Grade students to find whether the time of five months for a semester spent on them is proper. We found that only one month period is enough for that. Mathematically it can be said that only 20% of time, energy and resources are sufficient for the result. Then, what is the sense in forcing an infant into school for years and also wasting five months for a job of one month?

NO RESPECT FOR TEACHERS

In contemporary system of education there is no veneration for teachers. Our policy makers think that teaching is a profession which, too, needs training. It is presumed that more the teachers, better the quality of education. The affluent institutions appoint specialist teachers. It is presumed that less the number of students, more is the attention bestowed upon each of them.

Most of the contemporary educationists support this thesis. The students are the sufferers. Whom should they bestow their devotion upon? Each of the teachers, coming into the class, wishes to command the respect most. As a result, the tussle starts among the teachers for winning favour of the students. Consequently, the politics takes upper hand in relations among the teachers and the taught and the teaching suffers.

EXPERIENCE OF TEACHERS IS NOT GIVEN DUE RECOGNITION

As far as the teacher is concerned, the training is expected from him, not the experience. The young person, who is a novice to this crafty world, has no experience of good and bad. What the child will learn from such a teacher! He cannot stimulate confidence in the students. It is no surprise that after enjoying so many facilities, the student learns a little. As such, he, unwillingly, turns up to be a supporter of the system of exploitation.

USELESS SYLLABUS

The information collected at the school has little relevance to day-to-day life. Even the languages have little use for routine communication. Irrespective of it, the student is asked to be proud of his collection of information and knowledge. Is it not shameful that before acquiring sufficient command over mother tongue, the student is forced to learn foreign languages? The mathematics he learns at school neither makes him adept with the vegetable vendors nor capable of keeping accounts in the office. History book contains chapters on personalities and incidents unrelated to him. He does not have any knowledge of rivers and mountains, forests and plains around. We do not teach things which deserve to be taught, but show our seriousness in teaching subjects having little relevance for life.

There is no seriousness in teaching professional and technical courses, too. No sufficient facilities are available for their teaching and experiments. Some educationists think that limited syllabus will provide ample chances for thorough coaching. But the problem seeks different answer.

DENIAL OF INDIVIDUAL ABILITIES AND FOCUS ON IMPRACTICAL IDEALS

In fact, the reason of the sorry state of contemporary education is overlooking of the realities of life and forcing upon students irrelevant ideals and asking them to work translate them in reality. Everyone is expected to fulfill the expectations. Those who cannot do are degraded as incapable and spineless.

How unfortunate is it that some Rama, Krishna, Buddha, Christ or Gandhi is our ideal. The new generation is tutored to accept it. It has no freedom or facility to argue. In fact, before such questions start taking shape, the young mind is already turned idle and fettered into discipline. If a Gandhi or a Buddha is the height of human progress, the idea of flourishing is meaningless.

WHO IS RESPONSIBLE FOR THIS SAD PLIGHT?

Who is responsible for the sad plight of contemporary state of education? Is it not the modern state of education itself? While accusing it, many facts appear before us. Today, a student is devoting his full time to studies. There are well furnished class rooms and school buildings. The mechanization has arranged innumerable facilities, including study material in low cost. Mostly, the teachers are trained. The students have little to worry about. The poor and the needy students are being given help in the form of scholarships, etc. so that they need not worry for other mundane needs of life. Why is it so that after so many facilities available, the modern education is in such a dismal state?

BETTER EDUCATION WITHOUT ADEQUATE FACILITIES IN ANCIENT INDIA

It is said that there was better education without adequate facilities in ancient India. It was imparted in the forest abode of 75+ years old teachers. Scant were the facilities there in the forest. Even for the bare necessities of life, the students had to beg. They had to attend to all the household chores of the teacher. They used to collect fresh firewood for sacrificial fire early in the morning, take the cowherds to the grass-fields for grazing. Where was the leisure there for studies? The teacher often used to go to bed late in the night and get up early in the morning. The students had, as the common practice of the age, to go to bed after the teacher had slept and get up earlier than him. The little time they could spare was not sufficient for all the students to have direct communication with the teacher. The seniors used to avail of this opportunity. The juniors had not only to do all the household chores but also to serve the seniors.

Even for learning alphabet, the newcomers had to serve their seniors. In fact, in those days, the path of learning was a journey of hardships. After overcoming all these obstacles, the students used to get mastery over not only on languages but almost all the important eighteen branches of knowledge, including Meemansa (the art of analysis), Nyay-Shastra (Logic), Ayurveda (knowledge of medicine and surgery), Dhanurveda (knowledge of handling weapons), Gandharvaveda (knowledge of dance, drama and music) and Arthashastra (Polity) in 15 to 18 years. At the time of entering the domestic stage of life, the student was healthy physically and mentally and possessed the experiences of facing and winning over the practical difficulties of life.

REFLECTIONS ON ALTERNATIVE SYSTEM OF EDUCATION

The system of education, negating personality of child, will not be helpful for flourishing of life. The knowledge of alphabet or the expertise in operating machines or knowing the basics of professions are foundation only. The alternative order we are contemplating about, will give man the opportunity of total development of his individual and social life.

RESPECT FOR INDIVIDUALITY

The society is formed by individuals. Society never comes to an end. It is the individual who dies. Therefore, the individual is predominant. That predominance presupposes respect for individuality. And, that respect has ingrained freedom to decide about oneself. It is a part of his being.

NEED TO LEARN

Till the student feels the need to learn, sending him to school will not be helpful. It may be harmful. The need to learn anticipates some preparedness. The child is readying himself in his pastime of singing and dancing, laughing and crying, loving and fighting. Sending child to school without any preparations will force him to learn the things which he does not need and not be able to concentrate upon subjects taught there. All of us know the young child of a blacksmith can mould a metal plate better than most of engineering graduates do. The reason is the need felt by him while watching his father do so. We are sending our children to schools to be trained in engineering, medicine or law, without creating any need of it. The poor child is there to satisfy the wish of the parents!

UNDIVIDED LOYALTY TO TEACHER

Undivided loyalty to teacher is essential for learning. This generates an unflinching courage in the mind of student and he moves ahead with confidence. It is not necessary that he takes up the advised path, but whatever way he walks upon leads him to his goal.

STUDENTS SHOULD TAKE UP MONETARY RESPONSIBILITY OF TEACHERS

Only the experienced persons have moral right to be teachers. Such persons should teach as per their wish.

Except their moral obligation, no other constraints should be there. As far as their salary is concerned, the students should pay for it, in cash or kind. It is quite possible that the supporters of present system may ask how the poor children will be educated. In my opinion, the readiness of the poor to pay in kind may solve the problem.

If the teaching is entrusted to retired persons, the cost on education can be minimized. They have limited household responsibilities. At the most they have to support themselves. It will always be cheaper to look after such teachers. Besides, it will be a great boon in disguise. The old will be saved from the life of idleness and be given an opportunity of enjoying a meaningful active life in the company of budding youth! Who is the person, by nature, not a teacher in the ripe age?

A TEACHER IN EVERY HOUSE!

Today it is not practical to get a teacher even for fifty students. In some of the states of India, one-teacher schools are there which are conducting classes from standard one to seven. Since there are old people almost in every house, every family has teachers! The better teachers in the locality will attract more students and a natural competition will balance the profession. It is somewhat akin to present tuition system but philosophically more sound and responsive.

TEACHER SHOULD UTILIZE SERVICES OF SENIOR STUDENTS TEACH JUNIORS

It is quite possible that a large number of students may be attracted towards a particular teacher. Should he appoint other teachers for assistance? No. Such appointments are an insult to the devotion of students. In such situation where the number of students is large, the teacher should utilize services of his senior students and make them teach the juniors. The teacher himself should concentrate upon seniors and supervise the teaching of juniors. In this way a single teacher can teach a large number of students. The standard of education will not suffer. In fact, the students who are entrusted the task of teaching to juniors get the opportunity of imparting their knowledge. They love it and prove themselves good teachers. I have conducted such experiments at my Academy and got promising response.

SYLLABUS HAS BEEN SOMEWHAT SIMILAR SINCE TIME IMMEMORIAL

A question may be raised about syllabus. How will it be worked out? In fact, the common subjects and their contents are known to everyone. The syllabus has been somewhat similar throughout the ages. It will remain so in the future as well. No syllabus is successfully pursued today because of the teachers, who, neither possess sufficient experience nor command adequate respect.

LIBRARIES AND THE LABORATORIES TO BE RUN BY ENTREPRENEURS

There is possibility of such a decentralized system of education getting impotent without having direct facilities of libraries and laboratories. As far as the libraries are concerned they are used a little at present. And, except the laboratories of science, others are seldom used. In the better system of education, the libraries and the laboratories will be needed. The entrepreneurs can organize them as business establishments and lend the facilities.

INSPIRING TEACHER MAKES STUDENTS ACQUIRE KNOWLEDGE

The teacher is there not to teach but inspire students acquire knowledge. The inspiring capacity is important. The inspiring teacher does not interfere in the dreams of his students. He even does not go for the evaluation of the chosen path of his students. His task is limited to making students realize that the work alone leads to the realization of the chosen path and he is always there as a friend, philosopher and guide. Once it is achieved, there is no need of teaching in the conventional sense of the term. There is no need of even expertise from such teachers. It is the confidence of the taught reposed in teachers which makes them worthy to be teachers! For the inspired students, the world is a large library and laboratory. Everyone is a teacher. The experienced and the revered teachers have the capacity to inspire.

STUDENTS SHOULD CHOOSE THEIR TEACHERS

But, who is to decide whether a teacher possesses the inspiring capacity or some examining body should be there to decide about it? Each of the students has to decide himself. His own experiences guide him, his mistakes enlighten him. The societies which are intolerant to mistakes hardly help create something meaningful. It is common knowledge that seldom does somebody learn from other's experiences. Even the child does not do it. He does not accept the burning nature of fire till he gets burns. Those who possess the experience of grazing cattle do know that even the animals prefer their own judgment. Then, what is the teaching worth for? Is the teacher for teaching? Teaching is meaningless. The work of a teacher is not to teach but inspire students to learn. And, an inspired student learns and reaches the pinnacle of his growth.

PERFECTION ACHIEVED

The youth, who, since his childhood, is always living in an awakened state of mind, is experienced of decision-making and braving the consequences of judgments at every step of life, for him the life is meaningful in all circumstances. He cannot have any complaints against anyone. The education of such a person flourishes the supreme possibilities of his being and he achieves the highest growth of his life!

ABODE OF KNOWLEDGE

It is an allegory written by the author long ago. The Abode of Knowledge is residence of Sage Pre De where inmates are busy in getting up-to-date knowledge in a remote settlement at mountain Gagarchula in the Himalayan foothills. The Abode resembles the ancient Gurukuls of India.

According to Indian tradition, life is divided into four parts, which are called Ashramas, i.e., Brahmacharya, Grihastha, Vanprastha and Sanyas. During the Brahmacharyashram, the young ones have to acquire knowledge. It is up to 25 years of age. Afterwards, one enters the household phase of life; marries, raises family and fulfills the related responsibilities. This phase is known as Grihasthashram. It lasts at 50 years of age. From 51 years starts Vanprasthashram, when the household person gradually abandons his responsibilities and transfers them to his offspring. It is up to 75 years of age. The last stage starts at 76 years and is known as Sanyasashram. At this stage, a person leaves his home and lives a life of renunciation in the forest. Such recluses used to run the schools known as Gurukuls. Often the couple comprising husband and wife was there, but the death of one did not hinder the running of the Gurukul.

The following description is not a story of an ancient Gurukul. It is a modern version of it known as 'Abode of Knowledge' which is being visited by ascetic Aniket and Dr. Akhilesh wandering in search of a centre where comprehensive knowledge is achieved without losing anything.

DROWSINESS BROKE

It was a mere coincidence that the drowsiness of ascetic Aniket and Dr. Akhilesh was broken together. They found themselves lying side by side on the way to Chhin Mountain.

The curiosity to know one another was natural. They opened their mouths simultaneously. But it looked as if they uttered words with great difficulty. What a surprise! Their uttering proved somewhat meaningless. After listening 'Aham Asmi' (I am) a number of times, Dr. Adhilesh could recollect that he had studied a language called Sanskrit in his primary classes. The language of the gods! Was the other person a god? Aham Asmi, I am...

The circumstances are the best teachers. After a couple of hours, both of them were conversing in Sanskrit language.

ASCETIC ANIKET

Ascetic Aniket told that he learned Sanskrit and Prakrit languages under the guidance of a learned teacher at the Mandarachal hill. He got mastery over eighteen branches of knowledge. But the wish to have more made him quit the Ashram of his master and proceed towards north. After travelling months together, he fell down unconscious. It was then that a deep sound awoke him.

DR. AKHILESH

"What do you say? A deep sound? I am also awakened by it. After getting higher education in renowned foreign universities, I realized that I could get very little knowledge.

"Afterwards, I returned to India. Somebody told me that an educational institution is being run somewhere nearby for some time where real education is being imparted. I started looking for such an institution and went on walking and walking. At last so much was I exhausted that I fell down unconscious. Only now I have woken up."

IN SEARCH OF BETTER EDUCATION

"Akhilesh, I left my house at a very tender age. The revered master invested me with sacred thread and initiated me into an arduous course of life. It was begging even for daily food. We had not only to serve the master, but also make all the arrangements of our household, from collecting firewood to taking cowherds to jungle. Where was the leisure for studies? The master used to go to bed late in the night and get up early in the morning. The moral obligation forced us to go to bed only after the teacher had slept and get up before him. Somehow if we could manage some leisure, it was not possible to have a close proximity to the teacher. The seniors among us got the preference. The juniors had to serve the seniors also. Even for learning alphabet, we had to provide manual service. In this way, we had to make sacrifices for learning each of the letters of alphabet and words. That was the existing arrangement there. None was happy with that. Probably, the teacher, too, was not satisfied. One day he called us. While putting forth his point of view, he told a story. I do not know whether it was a true one, but it forced me to decide leave the Ashram of the master permanently in search of better system of acquiring knowledge".

LEGENDRY EXPERIMENT IN EDUCATION

"The master told thus – The pupils of great Himalayan sages Gauri and Khimuli, Sages Premu and Debuli, were popular and revolutionary teachers of their time. A number of students were studying in their Gurukul. Their love for Brahmachari Shwetketu was special. He was a stubborn and willful lad. The Sages wished him to be a versatile genius. But the education available in their Ashram was not deemed to be sufficient for Shwetketu. Sage Premu visited other seminaries to study the system of education there, discussed it with other learned sages. But he could not find any seminary suitable for Shwetketu. At last Premu and Debuli launched a new system of education in their Ashram.

"Some of the huts of the Gurukul were vacated. The learned scholars of all the important branches of knowledge were invited for teaching. The students were provided with reeds, ink and thin bark of Bhoj tree for writing. The classes were conducted from sunrise to sunset. Only leisure time was there for mid-day meal.

"The experiment got wide publicity even in those days of limited propaganda channels. Many of the neighboring Gurukuls started copying and delivering the same type of education. But, whereas before the experiment, only Shwetketu was a problem, now almost all the participating students turned up to be so. Their willful attitude started showing the traits of stubbornness and arrogance. The education did not hold much importance for them. None of the eighteen branches of knowledge impressed them much. Except the Sages Premu and Debuli, other teachers were treated shabbily.

"Sages Premu and Debuli were very much disappointed and frightened and consequently one day they closed down the experimental Gurukul".

SUBMISSION OF ASCETIC ANIKET

"Akhilesh, there was no limit to our surprise to see tears rolling down from the cheeks of our master while narrating the story. Do you know, what he said at last? He told that Sage Premu accepted his defeat. Probably he had not had enough courage to take the experiment to its logical end. Otherwise, he would have had got the glimpse of a golden future. At that time, the master asked if there was someone among us who could carry on the experiment of Sages Premu and Debuli.

"I stood up with folded hands, in submissive posture. Since then, I could not take any rest."

"Akhilesh, to get education without wasting life is really a great dream. Let us get up and find out the school giving such type of education."

"But Aniket, this ardous long journey has turned me doubtful about the existence of any such institution. Our labor may go wasted."

"Yes, it is possible. This attempt may also prove futile. But, we are two now!"

NORTHWARD JOURNEY

Both the hermits together walked on towards the direction the sound emanated from. There were a number of obstacles on the way. Somehow with tottering steps and escaping from ferocious wild animals, they reached at the top of Chhina peak in the evening.

No sooner did they look at the vast terrain below, spreading over in the north, they felt relieved.

LEGEND TO EASE THE BORING WAIT

The sudden unexpected sight of the landscape made them to postpone their journey for the day. They collected some eatable roots to satisfy their hunger and rested under a pine tree for the night. But, next day they got up very early in the morning and waited for sunrise.

"Aniket, the wait is always boring. As a past time, I would like to tell you a story I have heard in my childhood from my grandmother.

"There was a beautiful young woman, habitual of making herself up nicely for show off. Once she decided to go to the periodic village fair. Therefore, the previous night, after the dinner, she preferred to make her up first for the next day fair and not to wash the utensils. After finishing up with the job, she came out of her house to find how much time was left for the morning. The innumerable stars were twinkling in the sky. The morning star had still not risen on the eastern horizon. She kept on taking rounds of the courtyard. At last tired of such visits, she sat down at the hearth quite sleepy. She dozed off and fell on the ground head on. Somehow, she managed herself, got up and continued with her wait.

"In the morning, she was the first woman on her way to the fair. But whoever saw her face started laughing. She was happy that her wakefulness had brought good results. But a crazy young lad could not control himself.

"O sister-in-law, did you look at the mirror before stepping out of the house?"

"Why darling! The real beauty doesn't need any mirror."

The naughty lad, quickly, put the mirror before her eyes. What a surprise! The fair lady's face was blackened. When, where and how, she herself was not aware of it!"

IN THE ABODE OF KNOWLEDGE

With the first rays of sun in the morning, the northern terrain was engulfed in sweet music of flute, followed by combined ringing sound of trumpets, bells, drums and other musical instruments. For some time not only the area but the total surrounding was humming with sweet sound. While enjoying it, the hermits were on their feet again.

"Welcome to the Abode of Knowledge", uttering this, a young lad greeted them. It was self-evident that that person was a native of the settlement. But, his appearance, mannerisms, language and clothing did not vouch for his being either a worker or a master. He did not look like a businessman, too. Nor was there any sign of a student. He was walking with firm steps. There was no exhibition in his behavior. The delivery of words was restrained but forceful, personality confident.

"What is this settlement called?" Dr. Akhilesh enquired.

"It's not an ordinary settlement. It is an Abode of Knowledge!"

"We have come to know that there is a center of learning somewhere at the foothill here, where it is possible to acquire knowledge without wasting life. Is it the same centre?"

"This is the only educational complex around. If you are interested in discussion on a novel system of education, you may very well meet sage Pre De, the inspirer and initiator of this Abode. He is available at the hutment over there."

CITY OF KNOWLEDGE BUT NO STUDENTS AROUND

Both the hermits proceeded ahead. Though resembling a city, how different was it altogether! Tidy and quiet streets, nicely arranged markets, on the one side the tiny mills and factories and on the other, the green and bloomy fields, gardens full of flowers and fruit-bearing bushes and trees. Men and women, even the little kids, were engrossed in their activities. The curious eyes could see enough, tried to understand and make out as much as it was possible, but could not see any educational centre running in a formal way.

"Aniket, what kind of an abode of knowledge it is! Nowhere are the students visible. Even the tiny tots are busy in productive labor. Is it not a medieval city untouched by modern civilization? But the state of affairs and available facilities present a different picture altogether. Look at the young man working with the powerful computer installed to the north of the facing factory. The children of his age may be studying hardly in 9th standard elsewhere".

"Akhilesh, the visitor need not to be swayed by emotions!"

"Don't you see each person here is working beyond his capacity?"

"Akhilesh, it is not so. I have been witness to such an engrossing labor."

AMONG THE CHILDREN

"Visitors are welcome! Please, interact with our tiny tots," said the master-like person there.

"Our little heroes, please, greet the visitors. Know the outside world through them. (Pointing to ascetic Aniket, the master-like person says) Look, our ancestors in the past looked like him and now, the people of the world are like him (pointing to Dr. Akhilesh). (Facing them) Sirs, our children would like to be acquainted with you."

Both of them gave their brief introduction and informed them that they were on a journey to the Abode of Knowledge.

In yonder comes a child and asks, "Why have you grown your beard".

Another child, "Don't you know The Sage also sported a beard? The love hid itself behind it".

The first child, "Yes, the love was there playing hide-and- seeks. Haven't you seen as soon as The Sage meets us he is so lovable sometimes, but another times so much demanding?"

The third child, "Even if you give us sweets, we will not accept them right now. It's our work time." (Looking at the master-like person) "Isn't it so, Sir"?

As soon as the children got reminded of the work, they dispersed and joined their assignment.

"Who are these children?"

"They are our students."

"But, they are engaged in picking up pebbles on the road!"

"They are very small, can't do any other work."

"Are you their teacher?"

"Yes, for this month."

"Afterwards...?"

"Every month, our children get the opportunity of selecting their teachers. If they like so, I may remain their teacher afterwards also."

"Who bears the expenses incurred upon these children?"

"They themselves do it. They are reimbursed for their labor."

"What is about your emolument?"

"It is fixed up on the basis of work done by the students."

"Then, is it not possible that the teachers impose extra load of work on students for getting more emolument?"

"It is possible. But, the students will not turn up to you from the next month."

"All the teachers may join together to exploit students."

"Yes, it is also possible, but only when the nature of competition is worn out from the mind of teachers. It has not happened yet. We do not think it is practical with any animal of flesh and bones."

"When do the children study?"

"They are studying every moment. Probably, reading and writing is only education for you. For us, it is just a part of it. We do teach reading and writing. You have come here at right time. Tomorrow, it is convocation day of our Abode. The students, who have finished their education, will receive their certificates signed by Sage Pre De."

SAGE PRE DE

"Sir, you are very much individualistic. Is there none else, except Sage Pre De in this Abode of Knowledge?"

"Of course, there are. All have their names. We have given names to each of the streets and markets, roads, fields, granaries, houses, factories, to each of them. Will you like to listen to so many names? As far as the Sage is concerned, he is head of this family, initiator of this way of life. Individualism or socialism, we have no relation with. We are attached to life, which has its unity, diversity and individuality."

"We are getting more curious while talking with you."

"Honorable Guests, we shall have more discussion in the evening. Please, take rest in the guest house adjacent to the Sage's hut. Two of our students will help you reach there."

"We shall go there by ourselves. We would not like the students miss their work and lose their earning."

"The work is collective. The wages are given on the basis of total work performed and the money is distributed equally among the students. Therefore, the students accompanying you will not lose anything monetarily. Instead, they will get the opportunity of leading the strangers to their destination."

AT THE GUEST HOUSE

Both the hermits reached the hut- shaped dormitory of the Sage. They were greeted there by two well-built gate keepers at the entrance. A large hut was allotted to them for rest. The cupboards in the room were full of books on different branches of knowledge related to life and matter. The freshly published newspapers and periodicals were displayed on the tables. Some recreational material was also lying there.

No sooner did they reach there, a female assistant entered and requested them to wash up and get fresh. She helped them reach bathroom. Afterward, two other female attendants entered with fruits and drinks.

No sooner did they finish up eating, a male assistant informed that Sage Pre De himself was coming to meet them.

SAGE PRE DE ARRIVES

"Welcome Guests! I am Pre De", saying this, the Sage entered the room. An ordinary physique, carelessly shaved, wide forehead, shining eyes, nothing notable was there in that personality. For some time, ascetic Aniket and Dr. Akhilesh were wonder-struck. How could this person be an initiator of the Abode!

"Honorable Guests, we are thankful for your visit. The companions are waiting for you."

AMONGST THE ACADEMICIANS

Around twenty academicians were sitting in a room. They gave a standing ovation to the guests.

The Sage began, "Friends, two profound enquirers, ascetic Aniket and Dr. Akhilesh, will interact with you." He bowed down before all and went away.

The interaction began. One of the academicians conducted the meeting.

"Honorable Guests, we welcome you and show our readiness to clarify your doubts. Please, ask questions without any hesitation."

"We have heard that in the Abode of Knowledge one can get education without losing anything."

"Our student is not a prisoner, neither of an Abode nor of a class room for getting education. He himself selects the teacher, the subjects and the companions. He is the center of his group, which is the creation of his own selection. He alone is responsible for his selection."

"Is it not interference in his freedom to engage him in physical labor at this tender age?"

"To work is nature. It makes him self-dependent. How can it be harmful?"

"But, how is it possible to learn while doing physical labor?"

"Physical labor gives an opportunity to the worker to have direct contact with life and experience of solving its problems."

"What about reading and writing?"

"Very little is the role of reading and writing in real life. There is no need to sacrifice total prime time of active life for it. But, we do impart the knowledge of reading and writing"

"Have you had any definite syllabus?"

"No, but the systematic knowledge of the selected subjects is necessary. It is the teachers and their students who discuss and decide upon it."

"Do you hold any examinations?"

"Yes and no. At every stage, our student has to come up to the expectations of his teacher. But, at the same time, the student is free to go to another teacher with a proof of his attendance in the Abode; the proof of his attendance, not of the knowledge. The next teacher is free to take his entrance test before admission, may deny admission. A teacher can directly admit any child as his student also. As far as declaring result of the student is concerned, a committee is working directly under the supervision of the Sage. It takes the final test. On its recommendations, a student is declared as successful."

"Is it not possible that either the student or the teacher may turn up corrupt?"

"It is possible. The teacher can be bribed. The Sage himself may commit mistakes. If it happens often, we shall have to work for alternative. Since, from the very beginning, we teach the students to live self-dependent life, there are not many opportunities for corruption to raise its head."

"We could not see any school-like activities in the Abode of Knowledge!"

"There is no school being run in conventional sense here. As soon as the student enters Abode, he is engaged in earning activities first. Afterward, he is given assignments for knowledge. There are sufficient facilities for achieving mastery on chosen subjects. If the need arises, the student may be sent out for references. But, mostly we do not encourage it. Our emphasis is on providing him with total education of his choice here. You may be surprised to know that there is no paid worker employed here. The teachers and their students are two kinds of people present here."

"Do you consider some subjects more important than others?"

"Yes, the man is dumb without proper knowledge of languages. Therefore, languages are important. History gives the base to stand upon. Geography connects him with the life and matter around. Mathematics is useful for logical understanding. Science teaches the secrets of the cause and the effect. But, only these subjects are not important. Everything is essential which flourishes life, creates faith on it and does not take death as the end of life."

"One more question. Do you have any special method to find out the taste of students?"

"No. the fact is that it is the nature of man to express himself. We deduct his taste from it".

LIFE NEEDS FLOW, SAYS SAGE PRE DE

Next morning with the rise of the sun, the hermits were requested to attend the convocation where the fresh graduates were to be conferred upon the certificates of their successful education.

Ascetic Aniket and Dr. Akhilesh could not trust their eyes when they saw the persons sitting in the first row on the dais were none others than the attendants serving them sincerely since their arrival there! Soon after, they could hear the deep voice of Sage Pre De–

"Our fresh graduates, the world is waiting for you. Life needs flow. Maintain it. Let the ideals not confuse you. Let the faith in life grow because of you. Carry on your journey uninterrupted. Let the peace, peace alone, prevail!"

MUSINGS

To muse is natural. Some of the musings are given here as they represent the mind of the writer and may be helpful in understanding the treatise on alternative social order.

- Except the power of inspiration, all other powers are for dominance, forcing others to obey, to submit and act according to the whims of the powerful. As soon as the other collects necessary strength to disobey, revolts.
- I know you argue nicely. But it does not mean that what you say is correct. The truth is reality, not argument
- One of the most difficult things is communication. It is the first and the last step towards success. But, it is seldom possible. Therefore, people take up the path of violence. The non-violent method gives importance to others. It is the freedom of others to obey or not to. But, by violence one can accomplish what one wishes and can force others to be a means to his ends.
- Competition, victory and happiness. Competition, defeat and sorrow. Competition cannot be for its own sake. It is always for defeating others. If one is victorious, one is happy; if loses, sorrowful. Rise above competition and enjoy.

- Enjoy the work, even if you do not like it. Enjoy the 'not liking' of it.
- The truth mostly I talk about is known to many. But the necessary focus is not put upon it by them or it does not get necessary repetition. I do that.
- Everyone wants to avoid work. To train oneself to love it will make one accomplish something useful in life.
- No bride is beautiful after 3-4 days of her marriage. Afterwards, her work is appreciated, not looks.
- I often talk of making my children job-generators. Suppose, all turned up to be so, what will happen then? The guild of like-minded will take shape and a society of masters will come into existence.
- The problem with the language is its nature of generalization. Even the simplest of the simple facts cannot free themselves from it. A better mode of communication is still a dream.
- The thought of localized politics makes me scared. What will happen if a small village is divided and each of its parts expects to be given preference on the name of localized politics? No development is possible there. A poor society will be that!
- The flag-bearers are 'either-or'. Either they are an awakened lot or a bunch of slaves.

- Nobody knows who exploits whom for one's self-interest. All the famous names are just pawns in the hands of the corrupted.
- The much glamorized Rotary Clubs, Lions Clubs, etc. enjoy to be addressed as social service providers. In reality they do very little for society. They donate their left-over from the funds they collect for charity. The society must seek alternative arrangements for helping its social causes.
- One of our Smritikaras says–

Udyamah sahasam dhairyam buddhih shaktih parakramah
Shadete yatra vartante tatra deva sahaykrit

- Hard work, courage, patience, intellect, strength and valor, wherever these six are present, the god is there to help. But, there is no mention of Nishtha (devotion). Without it every quality is impotent.
- Son like the father, daughter like the mother! So much similarity is there. But each one is unique. This is individuality.
- "The mediocre teacher tells, the good teacher explains, the superior teacher demonstrates. The great teacher inspires!"
- Teaching is not science. It is an art, the art of communication.
- It is really a grave problem that one-sided success empowers one to guide multi-faceted life.

- The horse and the donkey. There is only one difference between the two. The horse knows the target, the donkey doesn't.
- The thought is important, not the language. If the thought is genuine and honest, any language will do.
- The mercy and the compassion. While showing mercy, one is always selective. In compassion, one is ready to surrender whatever one has. One turns up like a fruit-bearing tree or a river.
- The seeing presupposes two conditions – the presence of a thing and the light. Only one is not sufficient.
- Logic is useful but to a certain degree only.
- To dream is life. To realize the dream is happiness. To stop dreaming is death.
- The greatness does not run a race. If one is aware of one's capacities and has necessary confidence, one can achieve the desired end without running any race.
- So much sorrow, so much suffering, so much want and poverty is there that to me all the greatness sounds sponsored, the hailing cry of the oppressed, the lazy and the selfish. It is shameful that the fake greatness is hailed as the savior!
- Simplicity is natural. To remain so is penance.
- For thousands of years the life is facing the problem of food, cloth and shelter. The progress

has only created additional problems of water and air. What a sorry state of human progress!

- Most of us are beggars. Even saying prayers is an act of it.
- The problem with thinking is, it leaves implementation to others.
- The insulted can compose epics, not philosophies of life. The Valmikis, the Kalidasas, the Gandhis cannot be impartial to their judgments.
- There is little need of ornamental language for expressing thoughts.
- None is free from one's emotions.
- "Sow seeds if you are planning for the fruit within months; if within 20 years, plant a tree. But if you can wait 100 years, educate the generations!"
- Man does not live by bread alone. It is true. It is equally true that he cannot live without bread.
- Only the beggar can maintain his pride, he has no masters.
- It someone is not ready to accept defeat, you cannot defeat him.
- Often I am asked why a person with meager means like me goes for experiments for better social order. The answer is – Because the persons having sufficient means are not ready for it.
- The duality is world. The conscious of it is life. To accept it as it is, is pleasure and detachment from it is bliss.

- You have to execute the basic activities yourself. You yourself have to breath, drink, eat, see, listen to, talk, smell, taste, touch, walk, move limbs, desecrate or produce children. None else can do it for you. Even your god is of no help there.
- A contract laborer's position and future is worse than a slave's. A slave is a bonded laborer and as such, his wellbeing is his master's self-interest. There is none behind a contract laborer. The universities like Harvard, Princeton, etc. on the name of employability are creating slaves!
- The happy man is he who has sufficient work for the day. As soon as he gets up, the work is there waiting to be executed. Because of the work, he enjoys food, rest, sleep, even dreams.
- Representation. None can represent your hunger, your awakening.
- No truth is final, even the mathematical one. The only eternal truth is your self-confidence. With the help of it, you can perform miracles.
- The idealist, whether he is Socrates or Thomas Moore, Marx or Gandhi, Hitler or Mao, his biggest weakness is his inability to understand the complications of human nature. May be, the ideals, in the beginning seem inspiring, the one-sided approach towards life makes them impractical and gives birth to helplessness.
- I feel like crying to see myself helpless in doing something positive for the welfare of the needy.

But, I am still hopeful. If the problem is there, the solution has to be.

- Many times violent movements are necessary when the common man is the sufferer and exploited, the official is selfish and robber, the leader is corrupt and sensual, the priest is ritualistic and the teacher is opportunist.
- How shameful is it that the enemy whom you fought against for generations, as soon as you earn victory over him, you find yourself what the enemy liked of making you.
- Theories do not inspire common man. For the successful journey of life unlimited optimism is necessary. The dry tenets of philosophy cannot provide it. The common man needs guarantee of success before proceeding ahead on the path of action. This guarantee can only be provided by the stories of the successful.
- When you have nothing to say, not saying anything is the best policy of life.
- I am not a supporter of revolution. It is one-sided thinking, a belief in embracing the alternative. How can such thinking be for the welfare and happiness of all? I do not accept 'Sarvodaya' also. I wish welfare of all, good of all in stipulated time. It is possible in an emotion-bound society only.
- The worst type of helplessness of a thought-process is that it wishes to be a broad highway before becoming a pavement for the common

man. One day, even the thought-process will have to learn from its experiences.

- One day I paid a visit to a dormitory for the blind. Due to carelessness, I dashed into a stool and started moaning. All the blind in the room reacted simultaneously, "Sir, how careless are the authorities for our wellbeing! They cannot even light a bulb for us". The hall was shining in the light of a hundred watt bulb! I could not react as I was in minority.
- Whatever you are, it is because of your work, the work done by you or your forefathers. If you want to be something else, work for it.
- What you call education is just imparting some information, teaching some techniques. The real education liberates, inspires one to stand on one's own feet.
- Work individually in a group so that you can maintain your identity as well as remain connected to the society.
- Growth of human beings is better achieved by focusing on creativity, not on employability. Emotion-bound society is conducive to honor creativity. All others are mostly interested in producing obedient servants, not judgment owning masters!